S0-ARA-048

SCIENCE SAFETY
Being Careful

by Lionel Bender   illustrated by Jon Davis

PICTURE WINDOW BOOKS
www.picturewindowbooks.com

Thanks to our advisers for their expertise, research, and advice:

Dr. Stanley P. Jones, Assistant Director
NASA-sponsored Classroom of the Future Program

Susan Kesselring, M.A., Literacy Educator
Rosemount–Apple Valley–Eagan (Minnesota) School District

Editors: Jacqueline Wolfe and Nick Healy
Designer: Ben White
Page Production: Joseph Anderson
Creative Director: Keith Griffin
Editorial Director: Carol Jones
The illustrations in this book were created digitally.

This book was produced for Picture Window Books by
Bender Richardson White, U.K.

Picture Window Books
5115 Excelsior Boulevard
Suite 232
Minneapolis, MN 55416
877-845-8392
www.picturewindowbooks.com

Library of Congress Cataloging-in-Publication Data
Bender, Lionel.
Science safety : being careful / by Lionel Bender ; illustrated by Jon Davis.
p. cm. — (Amazing science)
Includes bibliographical references and index.
ISBN-13: 978-1-4048-2198-9 (hardcover)
ISBN-10: 1-4048-2198-8 (hardcover)
1. Science—Study and teaching—United States—Juvenile literature.
2. Science rooms and equipment—United States—Safety measures—
Juvenile literature. 3. Laboratories—United States—Safety measures—
Juvenile literature. I. Davis, Jon, ill. II. Title. III. Series.
Q183.3.A1.B463 2007
502.8'9—dc22   2006012127

Table of Contents

All About Science

Studying science is fun. You learn about the world around you. When you do science tests and investigations, you must be careful. There are simple safety rules to follow.

Experiments can be dangerous. Scientists know that science safety is very important.

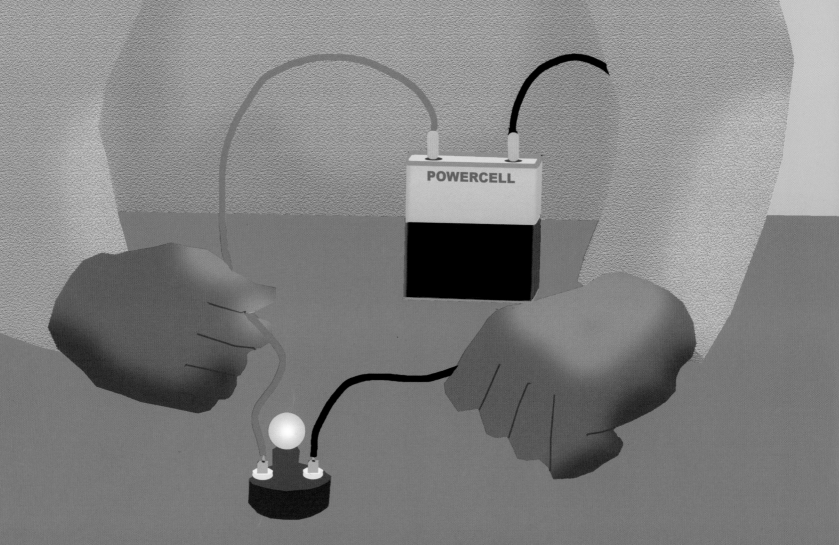

FUN FACT

Biology is the science of living things. Geology is the science of rocks and Earth's surface. Astronomy is the science of the planets and stars. What other sciences do you know?

POWERCELL

WATER

OIL

Safety Clothing

When you are performing experiments, put on goggles to protect your eyes. Wear an apron or a laboratory coat to keep your clothes clean. Wear plastic or thick gloves to protect your hands.

If you have long hair, wear a hat or cap or tie your hair back. If you are doing experiments outside, wear weatherproof clothing and gear.

Adult Help

Some science experiments may be dangerous. Adults must hold hot things with tongs or oven mitts. You can watch these experiments from a safe distance.

Let heated things cool down completely before you touch them. You don't want to get burned. Things that are very cold can burn your skin, too. Let them warm up first.

FUN FACT
Scientists often use robots to do experiments with heat. A robot is a machine controlled by computers.

Safety with Light

You can study light using a flashlight, mirrors, and lenses. Light is a type of energy. Very bright light can harm your eyes. To be safe, wear darkened safety glasses or sunglasses. Don't shine the flashlight in anyone's eyes.

Sunlight can burn your skin and your eyes. Never look directly at the sun. If you are studying outdoors on a sunny day, put on some sunblock and wear a hat.

Safety with Plants

When working with soil and plants, keep dirty fingers away from your mouth and eyes. Some plants are poisonous. Do not taste any plant material, such as berries, without asking an adult first.

Garden soil contains lots of small insects and bacteria. Garden plants may carry tiny pests. Clean your hands and your tools after studying the plants and soil.

FUN FACT

Humus is the part of soil that contains nutrients plants need to grow. You can grow plants without using soil, but you must add liquid plant food to the water in which they grow.

Safety in the Wild

When investigating ponds and rock pools by the water, beware of the waves and tides. An adult must be with you at all times. Use plastic jars to collect small animals. Write labels with details of what you collected, and put these on the jars.

When you study nature at school or at home, be sure to clean up when you are finished. Mop up any spills, and use disinfectant to wipe surfaces. This will remove any germs.

FUN FACT
Some pond animals are smaller than the period at the end of this sentence.

Safety While Collecting

If your class is out collecting things to study, stay with your group. If you hurt yourself, ask for help. Your teacher should have a first aid kit.

Looking for things to study is fun. Be sure to wear goggles to protect your eyes and gloves to protect your hands.

FUN FACT

The weather wears away rock. Over the years, the action of wind, rain, and ice slowly changes rock into boulders, then pebbles and stones, and finally into tiny grains of sand.

17

Safety with Electricity

You can study electricity using small batteries, lightbulbs, bells, switches, and wire. Batteries produce small amounts of electricity. Electric outlets at home and at school produce large amounts of electricity.

Make sure your hands are dry before you touch anything. Keep your computer area clear of any liquids. If you spill any liquid, it could give you an electrical shock. Keep everything clean and dry.

Lightning is giant sparks of electricity. Tall
buildings have lightning rods. If lightning
strikes a building, the electricity passes
down the rod safely to the ground.

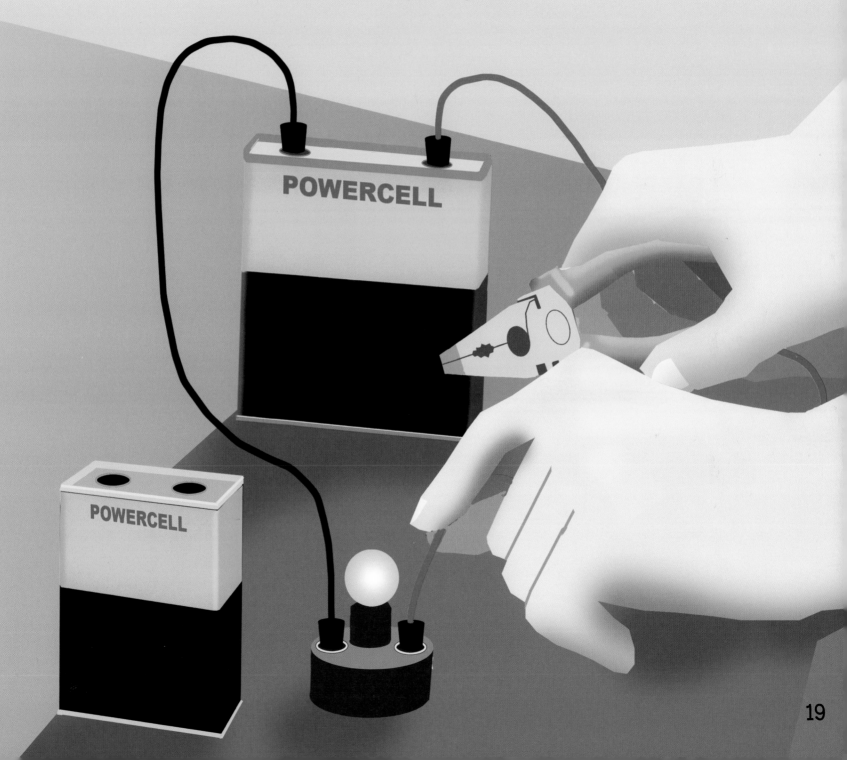

19

General Safety

Whatever science you are studying, follow simple safety rules. At school, follow instructions given by your science teacher. Pay attention to what you are doing. At home, always ask an adult to help you.

You can help with science safety, too. At home, ask your parents to have a safe, clean workspace. At school during experiments, tell your teacher or classmates if you see anything dangerous or harmful. Be safe, and have fun discovering the wonderful world of science.

Safety Posters

What you need:
- large sheets of paper
- colored pencils
- push pins

What you do:

1. Make a list of five safety topics and design a symbol you can use to illustrate each one. For example, you may choose protective clothing, fire, electricity, noise, water, and so on.

2. Write some safety rules to go with each symbol.

3. For each rule, write instructions for what to do if there is an accident.

4. Hang the posters on the classroom bulletin board.

Think about safety issues at your school and at home. Are there any places where accidents might happen? What can you do to make those places safer? What kinds of signs could you put up to warn people of the dangers? Do you know what to do if there is an accident?

Talk with your teachers and parents about these ideas.

Science Safety Facts

Robot Arms

At nuclear power stations, scientists use robot arms to handle dangerous materials. The scientists operate the arms from behind protective walls and windows.

Clean Air

Some scientists study germs. When they are doing so, they work in special rooms where the air is cleaned to remove any other germs. This way, the only germs are the specific ones the scientists are studying.

Rubber

Electricity does not flow through rubber. Scientists working with electricity wear rubber gloves and rubber boots to stop any injuries.

Gas Masks

Some gases are poisonous. Scientists wear special masks that contain filters that stop chemicals. Some gas masks also help prevent scientists from breathing in harmful germs.

Glossary

chemicals—substances made by or used in chemistry, which is the study of
   substances, what they are made of, and what happens when they are mixed
disinfectant—a substance that stops or slows the growth of tiny,
   disease-carrying organisms
electrical shock—a jolt of electric energy
experiment—a scientific test to see what happens if you take a certain action
germs—the earliest form of an organism; for example, a seed, bud, or spore
laboratory—a room where scientists do experiments, tests, and investigations
tides—the rising and falling of the ocean up and down the shore

To Learn More

At the Library

Freeman, Marcia S. *You Are a Scientist*. Vero Beach, Fla.: Rourke Pub., 2004.

Nye, Bill. *Bill Nye the Science Guy's Great Big Book of Tiny Germs*. New York: Hyperion Books for Children, 2005.

Robinson, Tom. *The Everything Kids' Science Experiments Book*. Holbrook, Mass.: Adams Media, 2001.

On the Web

FactHound offers a safe, fun way to find Web sites related to this book. All of the sites on FactHound have been researched by our staff.

1. Visit *www.facthound.com*
2. Type in this special code: **1404821988**
3. Click on the FETCH IT button.

Your trusty FactHound will fetch the best sites for you!

Index

Look for other books in the Amazing Science series:

Composting: Nature's Recyclers
   1-4048-2194-5
Erosion: Changing Earth's Surface
   1-4048-2195-3
Magnification: A Closer Look
   1-4048-2196-1
Science Measurements:
   How Heavy? How Long? How Hot?
   1-4048-2197-X
Science Tools:
   Using Machines and Instruments
   1-4048-2199-6